BONES TO BURY

To Pat
with best wishes

James Strecker
2010

BONES TO BURY

POEMS AND SCULPTURE BY

JAMES STRECKER

Photographs by Peter Hogan

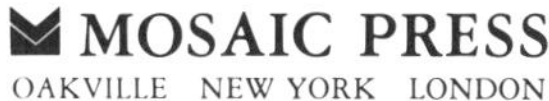

MOSAIC PRESS
OAKVILLE NEW YORK LONDON

```
Canadian Cataloguing in Publication Data

Strecker, James, 1943-
  Bones to bury

Poems.
ISBN 0-88962-249-3

I. Title.

PS8587.T73B66 1984      C811'.54      C84-098640-8
PR9199.3.S77B66 1984
```


Published by Mosaic Press, P.O. Box 1032, Oakville, Ontario, L6J 5E9, Canada.

Published with the assistance of the Canada Council and the Ontario Arts Council.

Copyright©James Strecker, 1984
Second Printing 1986

Design by Doug Frank
Typeset by Speed River Graphics
Printed and bound in Canada

ISBN 0-88962-249-3 paper

Distributed in the United States by Flatiron Books, 175 Fifth Avenue, Suite 814, New York, N.Y. 10010, U.S.A.

Distributed in the U.K. by John Calder (Publishers) Ltd., 18 Brewer Street, London, W1R 4AS, England.

Distributed in New Zealand and Australia by Pilgrims South Press, P.O. Box 5101, Dunedin, New Zealand.

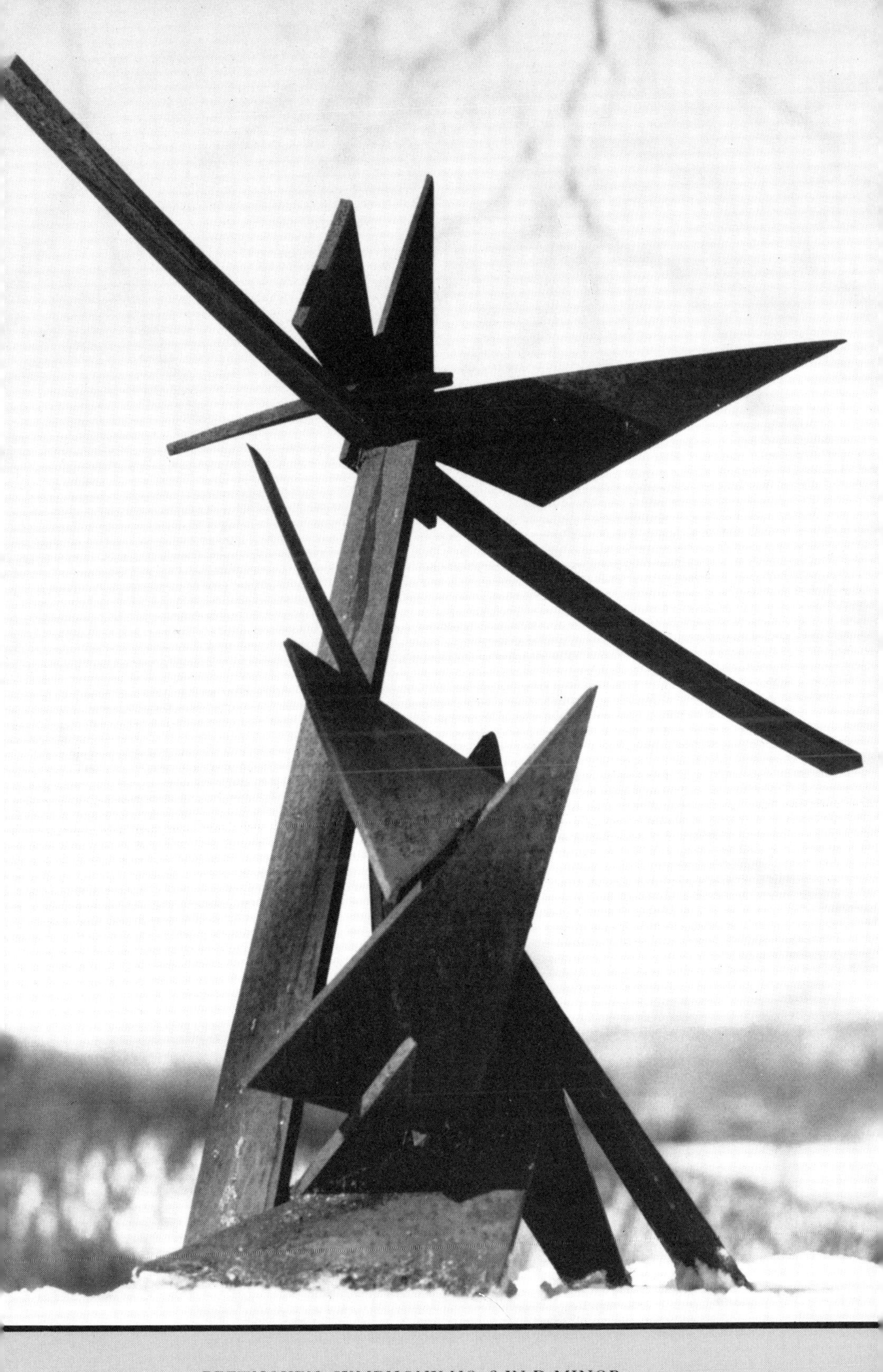

BEETHOVEN: SYMPHONY NO. 9 IN D MINOR

For Margaret
for Anna Tantala
for Pierre

Contents

BONES TO BURY

ALI MBAROC

We sailed from Lamu
in a dhow, Ali Mbaroc's;

the day ran out of breath
at noon. The piecemeal

wind let fall a dry caress
on our faces, then grew

passive, died like a
cloud unfolding. The Kenyan

sky was pure, eternal stuff;
it held us by the gut. I

was happy. Ali's singing
spiralled ashore in delicate

threads, strands of a tale
woven in smoke. He said the

words described a young girl.
She lived for a moment in

his voice where the words
of a song might unveil her.

INEFFABLE BEAUTY

To create
the pigment of

roses

for your cheek

living rabbits
were

tortured
in a lab; their

eyes were
burned away.

I have no word
to compare

your skin

to petals.

WASYL SZEWCZYK

This method I learned
from Charlie:

After the meal
wash your bowl and spoon.
Let them dry
on the counter
until you eat again.
Be patient.

He was a bachelor.
In his seventh decade
they brought women
like weatherbeaten cattle
to the timid man's home
for him to take
in marriage. He rejected
the sagging Polish
widows and their matchmade
schemes for his land.

He left the house and garden
in a will. There was little
else: four boxes of novels
describing sophisticated
bachelors and accessible blondes,
and a handful of age-ruined
photographs, the girl
beautiful in 1921.
Had he loved her?
He wanted to nod his head yes,
but couldn't.

He left an epithet, Charlie,
a handy anglicized substitute
for the alien Wasyl.

We removed two kinds of shirts
from his room: white shirts
covered with cellophane, then
dust (these should not be spoiled
too soon by common labourer's
use) and others laden with sweat,
odors of work eating the fibres.
He wasted nothing, not even
his life.

Wasyl Szewczyk is dead,
Wasyly Szewczyk of Galicia,

a Ukrainian serf from a feudal
age who despised the priest
and his landowner's god.
He had seen a pregnant girl
beaten by holy fists, had
fled to a dirty coal mining
town, a fourteen hour shift,
and wept from the pain
of his burned, bandaged hands.

His fingers learned to play
the clarinet, cut hair
with a barber's expertise,
hold a book of Shevchenko's
poetry. He was attuned, like
spring, to the delicacy
of creation.

At meals he belched with thanks,
a peasant.

He lies buried in Beausejour
Manitoba where he once pastured
cows, his hair as black
as a rainsoaked prairie field.

Wasyl   Szewczyk is dead.
There was little to say after him.
We lacked his wit, was it peasant
or Slavic, that taunted death
as a nuisance and friend.
He knew the dead to be lucky.

What aspect knows the man?

He posed unsmiling for photographs.
He lived a long life,
should have hated the world.
He wore a suit on Sundays.

Charlie Szewczyk, the farmer Wasyl,
died last April
in his eightieth year.

At seventy-five
he had learned to play
the violin.

THE SMELL OF ROSES

You are singular
among mannequins,

like no one
in particular.

You pour Chinese
tea; we sit on
your pillow. I

try to manipulate
your senses

but I maul your
breast instead.

A smell of roses
fills the air,

but it's stuff
from a can,
not roses.

A proud liturgy,

dirty hands carving
mountainous earth,
stone-ornamented haven
where gods endure
and summon minstrelsy.

Song erupts,
cloudburst in the making,
rips the trifling soul
apart. Music speaks
a mountain to the sea.

Let's not belabour
how wretched men are,
how open to hell
their rage without tears;
seasons abide the unjust.

For every moment of sorcery
another, singing, breaks
captivity's chain,
shouts matter of life
dividing.

In each man's public heart
voices drink a never-ending
well, and drag the
oppressor's idol of gold
into the sea.

QUAND LE BESOIN EST
PLUS FORT QUE LA PEUR
D'AVOIR BESOIN

J'ai peur
J'ai peur de toi
Touche pas mon coeur
Je t'en prie, ne meurs pas

à Margie Gillis

On the way to Auschwitz
the train stopped at
a Kentucky Fried Chicken stand.
Four thousand orders were
taken: the short-order cook
bitched about the lousy pay.

The train resumed its run
past Polish farmers
harvesting in the field. The
Jews in livestock cars
waved their pieces of chicken
wing, and sipped on icy cola
from wax-coated cups,

many had asked for two straws.

Word has it
the cleanup crew who swept
the debris all that night
had a hell of a time. The

floors were a mess: napkins,
withering cole slaw,
and piles of sticky bone
smelling of meat.

IN HIS WAY

before death
won him
crippled
and thirsty,
my grandfather
took decay
of the heart
for music;
he spread
his daughters
like tentacles
of a poor
man's harp
to grow
in a workingclass
slum.

old man
with haying fork
in hand,
he lost it all
so many times,
why stir
the brain
for dates? amen
to the blues of
an immigrant
who travels
unadorned:

he scraped
through
this world
where others
fell down,
an Orpheus
ascending
in his way.

HE WAS WOUNDS

He was wounds
waiting for a knife. No
fiend ran a dagger across
his tongue
to make a speechless
fool of him; he
stuttered and mumbled quite
on his own,
learned to undo
his fly. At dusk
when sunset crawled over
the waves to
welcome his aching feet, he
pissed a rushing, golden
arch, marvelled
at the rainbow. At dawn
he drank the water. He

was wounds
wounded in slavery. But
no blood dripped
from his servile
arm. He cut through
his skin every day
and with the advent of night
walked through the
hazy scent of pine,
pilgrim to the labourers'
camp. No one could find
his blood. The men all
took swings with
their axes too,
found their blades
as dry as his
wounds. He

was wounds
awaiting the turbulent
herd, hooves
to trample his head
near the barn. Only
a workhorse appeared, a
tired mare, weary
without any wounds. The
animal would not move.
He walked to the house,
picked up his hammer,
ran to the yard. He
beat at her ribs
till she bled with
a crack. The wounded
was looking
for wounds.

THE WOMAN LEFT A STRANGER

The fist: a stone
that separates

method from anger,
love
from everything else.

We stood on the sand
of Calais,
remembering lovers

and rock.

You held my body,
found the marrow

missing.

You touched me
with lamenting hands

and words
I could not shatter.

McLuhan, in Memoriam

Let us barter what we know
for the quiet bell unrung,

listen how laws of earth
come together in particular
lives. Then celebrate the

maker in man, the passion
for sense between ocean and
shore. A friend is dead.

He was born where the prairie
extends flat-bellied: no
place to wander false or
gutless among the stars.

A subtle imagination, he
riffed on academia, jazzman
to the tried and true.

Shall we remember celebrity,
the keynote sounded in musing
free, or how we sensed
midnight dividing in him?

McLuhan died in a winter
of many deaths. We miss
the unfolding truth of a

special man and his deus
ex machina, laughter.

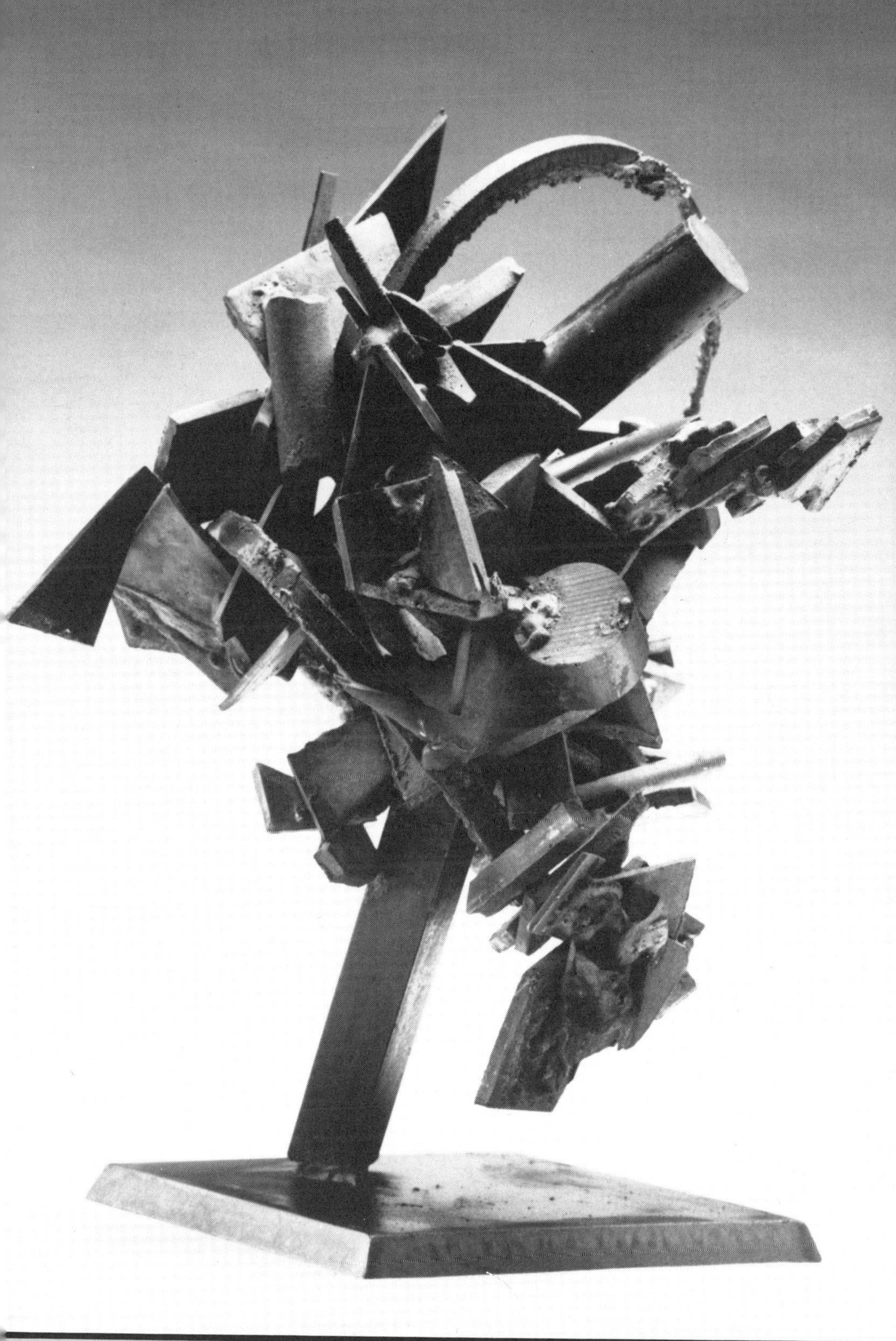

MEMORIAL TO McLUHAN

MARINA

perhaps she was a seawind
coasting
        above the sensuous,
    compelling young scholars to
quote poetry
        and they stole
           impassioned lines
to describe
    what she must have described
  many times
       for only one
        of them

perhaps she was a seawind,
knew
    they were seabound too
    the disciples who found her
in their
      inkstained hands
       and touched in her
what must be
    tried if coasting wind will give
  young men
      a midnight
        on the sea.

so loosened in performance,
cast
    from herself in love
    or sailor's destiny
imprisoned
      by their poetry,
       their waves
in stolen
    windy sea, she did give birth
  did love
    one love's profound
      conformity.

LA CAMARGUE

Twenty miles on foot
through the Camargue,
a prostrate land, austere
design; the wind and a rabid
sun compete for my brain.

I am seeking white horses.
Legend has it the herds
run free, but they don't;
ragged studs gather to weigh
the curse, another season.
Along the ditch, bushes
bowed like mendicants
bear the howling scoop
of Mediterranean wind
above, gouging gusts
mad and starving.

Then to walk the ramparts
of Arles, nothing more
lonely in this world
than midnight wind
in an ancient town, a river
flowing beside it. The
Rhone disappears
out of colour into the night;
I remember the chill
Gothic architecture
sends down the spine,
and how we are alone
with or without God. Then

to bed in a room of wooden
shutters, Cante Flamenco
rising from the square
into dreams I never describe
that put man and his
death together.

BIOG

To mine
his heart
you have to
dig banal.

Born
of a trifling
god, he
was allotted

a portion
of sin
and ordered
to screw

until
his ears
fell off. He
learned

to succeed;
when an ass
was bared
he puckered.

He married
a rose
whose dreams
turned

sons of bitches;
then
he clawed
at her, and

clawed at her,
he clawed
at her
with words.

MASAI MARA

The wildebeest flow
to Masai Mara
burst from Serengeti.
A lion, still as vapour
in the grasses,
watches over
the gnu's hungry surge
for another place.
He waits
with absolute balance,
a planet
in outer night. Death
and twilight
wait their turn
beside the feline
predator.

A rancid sky
when something dies,
milked of dignity.
Perhaps you understand
though what we know
is not the same. I
eat no meat,
kill in not killing.
And powerless to heal,
ten dreadful steps
from a lion
whose paw
might crush my throat,
I give the lion leeway,
not man.

Masai Mara, 1980

The hands you wipe
on flannel trousers,
the fingers you dry

with absolute care,
have embraced a universe.
Each bone has raged,

an epic in time,
slave owner and enslaved.
Your hands have brandished

axes, felled trees to build
a highway; they've held one
woman with terror, another

for revenge. The fingers are
cracked with workingman's
age, burned by industrial

fire. Each infinitesimal line
of dirt runs like a vein
blackened and sluttish,

smelling of iron, almost
diseased in dust. The nerve
endings feel ruined; a glass

of beer is clutched in keen
desperation, cigarettes
rolled too carefully, no

longer with impartial grace.
Now you smile slowly,
clumsily poking piano keys,

finding waltzes by Strauss
and hymns of weary gratitude
somewhere in your hands.

THE REWARD FOR NOT EATING MEAT

I admire the way
Miss Laura Antonelli

pays a bimonthly visit
to Toronto

in the nude. Whenever
she's in town

I take off my clothes
and grab a cab

to the Bloor Cinema
for a box of popcorn

and soda with ice. One
day, I prophesy, she'll

descend from the screen,
rest her ten foot

Technicolor bum
on my lap. Then she'll

whisper, soft as feathers,
in my ear:

"You smella so nice,
you sexy vegetarian!"

PARIS

I remember cities
with names,

my dead are dreaming
streets the watchmen see.

Memory or death,
from here a swimmer
looks to shore.

Down the alley
a ribbon of light
finds way,

weaves through the curtain
through your hair
and my mind,

two strangers and the night
in a rented room,
the hum of boulevards
a sea.

Your hair is brushed
in strands of starless night;

if you are still alive,
remember me.

THE NEW ARCHETYPAL STATE

What now King Oedipus?
Teiresias declines to play
his card. Jocasta is alive,
I saw her only yesterday,
kneeling inside the Theatre
of Dionysus, gazing
beyond the Acropolis,
guarding her love this time.
The modern Athenian man

was killing time in Omonia
Square, thumbing komboloia,
eyeing American girls
knapsacks dangling
over tight blue jeans.

And Crete did not embrace
your fated agony.
At a newsstand in Iraklion
I found your sins in
paperback, bought some aspirin
for a maddening pain in my eye.

We stayed a month in Crete,
my wife and I. One day,
guidebook in hand, we visited
the Lassithi Plateau
to pay our respects in a dank
and lonely cave where Zeus
was born. Zeus wasn't there
but we met a part time guide
from the village; he wanted
ninety drachmas
to show us around.

HOMECOMING

A city-bred farmer, virgin
to the plough, cursed long ago
the parched, ungiving earth.
He endured no ploughman's
temptation to bend his back
akin to supple fields
of Mantioba wheat.

I watched over him last April,
his dread and wisdom burned out;
darkness prevailed, master of the eye.

We stopped for gas. The
attendant's dog appeared and licked
my hand, whimpered, ran away.
The western sky shivered

a reply to Winnipeg lights;
around me, hushed, the farms
of Beausejour

where I lived, a child, until three,
where my ancestors rot
like stubble of wheat.

I accuse every child not aborted:
he gnaws on the sun cruelly.
Yet the charge refuses to vindicate
how we followed a gentle man's hearse,
parted the night with his coffin.

GULLS

Why gulls
when I think of my life
and the moon holds still?

they spur no criterion
but wonder.

When the sun is only a sun
betraying its echo
to night,
a gull remains like a star

a semblance of joy
I can't explain
told in beauty.

A gull hangs overhead,
tracing my inner,
more seasoned accord
with the seed of his life

in mine. Then night
closes in without a sigh
or lament

ebony voiced, footprints
of moon in the water.

for Ira Progoff

THE MAN WHO WANTED A SON

"This favour will make you
a man," he said

and he kicked me in the groin
as hard as any guy

doing a good turn.
Then he offered me his daughter.

She was faceless
and serene, elusive as a

field goal falling
through a cloud.

A ONE ROOM SHACK

a one room shack (
they do exist
) in 1946

my mother awoke
to see her gentle hand
turn arthritic claw

she yielded the farm,
bore the curse
of barely making

a living. in Washington
she posed her sons
beside the Capitol

preserved their faces
like strawberry jam.
then Hamilton,

choking industrial
fumes, though I try
to believe she simply

inhaled, let the smoke
pass through her
bones without

coagulating. in truth
she hardly stood her
ground. her mongrel dog

died; she quivered with
guilt to know she would
need then lose another.

VANESSA HARWOOD

Her body,
an exquisite throw
of dice, brings
tremor to the wind.

The ravenous cat
stalks an airy
prey.

She purrs a notion
for the kill,
flaunts
a genteel claw
embedded in velour.

A feline made coy,
daring to fly,

she reaches
to pilfer a drop
of ether's blood.

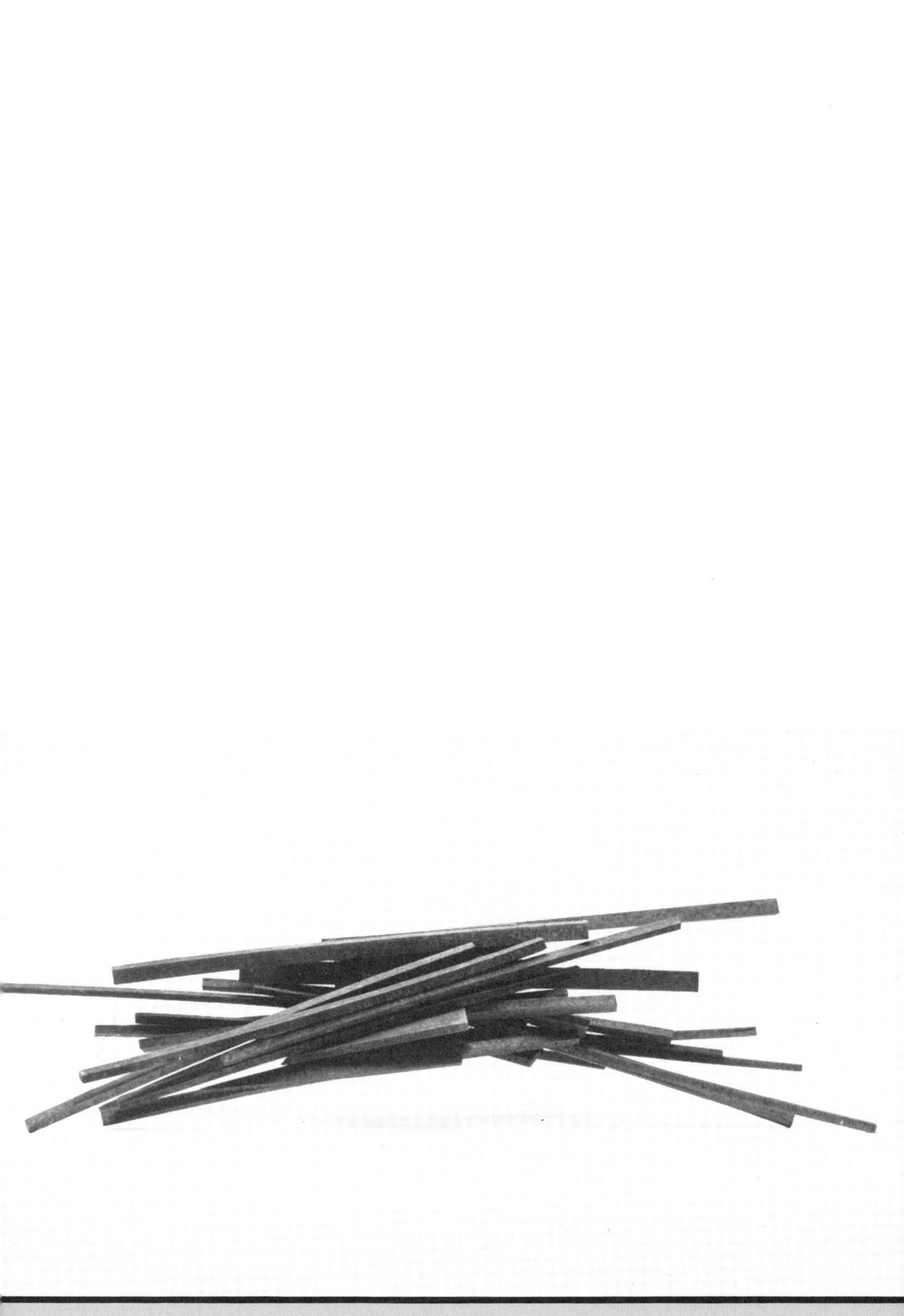

QUINTET

I

you bargain
with your eyes,
a taker taking
what she can.

I'm a tossup,
one side
of a coin
(your dime)

II

a quirk
of vanity: we
collect stones
for the mundane
vacuum
we fill.

at a jeweller's
window
you prefer
a diamond
harder than
steel.

I see
your reflection.
who cut
the first
diamond?
you, I suspect.

III

woman disguised,
floral pattern
dress, a
wreath too gaudy
for the dead:

it's autumn
in August,
who are you?

sleepless
as a lake
you conjure ways
to make me
sting.

IV

you stare,
penetrating eyes,
unnatural blue,
to uncover
what you
have become

moody fingers
reach under
your blouse.
you rip
your tit
asunder,
throw it
in my face.

V

your eye's
contempt,
my cigarette
butts, my
stuttering
gestures of the
hand:

you pounce,
an icy
vulturine wind
on a traveller
between towns.

THE UNIVERSITY GRAD

These half-digested
platitudes play havoc
with my skull. I stand

before a footnote-spewing
mouth attending wicked
whirlwinds of babble on.

Her judgement settles,
a satisfied slime, on
every damned thing!
She meditates two feet
                in front
                of herself
while her
brain is
trying to
c a t c h   u p.

AT 7:15 THIS MORNING
THE RCMP
SEIZED 8 KILOS
OF MEANDERING JARGON
FROM HER MOUTH

NO ARREST WAS MADE

IT HAD A STREET VALUE
OF 37¢

LES ARENES

The surrogate Nazi
asks me, a vegetarian,
to choose between
a confused, tormented
bull and my hypothetical
daughter. As if I were
a Gypsy or a Jew nursing
twins, insensibly
compelled to decide
the skull he'd crush
underfoot.

Let this be plain.
When the elegant matador's
knee starts to quiver
I shout "Good falling of guts!"
and cheer the bull.
I drag a spectator
idly diverted by death
to crude butchery on the curb,
carve his belly
for wandering bitches
on the Boulevard des Lices.

Then I light a candle
in the church of St. Trophime,
consider the contagion
of human curiosity. The
flickering light imposes
a grin on the skull
overhead, centuries old,
pockmarked with time,
carved when angels had to
jostle for standing room
on the head of a
picador's pin.

Arles, 1978

OFRA HARNOY

A gesture
draws goblin darkness
around her. She

sways upon the mind,

favours
the solitary pulse
desolate but infused

with every petal
of spring.

Who would think
a waterfall
might be here

pouring
reason's icon
into the wind?

Reason become
the ripening song intended,

she remains
not music or idea

but the haunting reach
of wonder.

St. Lawrence Hall, February 14, 1983

THE SQUIRREL

The squirrel fastens
September to March,
stuffing his cheeks
full of nuts
and seeds.

I take this glutting
of a belly
for esoteric laughter;
the squirrel girdles

his heart with fat,
gilds a death
he can't foresee.

Verdant leaves
abstract into autumn.
The squirrel chatters
near a tree

teases Sumitra, our
patient cat,
of scythelike spine
and cool, implosive
eyes.

WOMAN'S YEAR

The side of Adam
is stitched; a
woman emerges
from the womb
of Adam's Grandma.

It's your birthday,
heaven bless.

The angel of death
in a pin stripe
suit
conducts a press
conference. He
sweats upon
your declaration:
equal pay
and yoga.

It's your first
honest day,
the hour of yin
with a punch
and damn
the whore-spiced
madonna.

The macho
fruit of karma
looks meekly
through the keyhole
of your cross;

he calls you
a hyper bitch.

THE DEATH OF GLENN GOULD

Now it opens to winter,
the fire lit in solitude.

The photograph shows
a soul's privacy, perfect
yet passing, his dream
unready for sleep.

What dream in this coffin?
The man's compassion for
animals akin to formal
ecstasies of Bach? We

mourners bring soul's scrutiny
to his beauty like a stem.

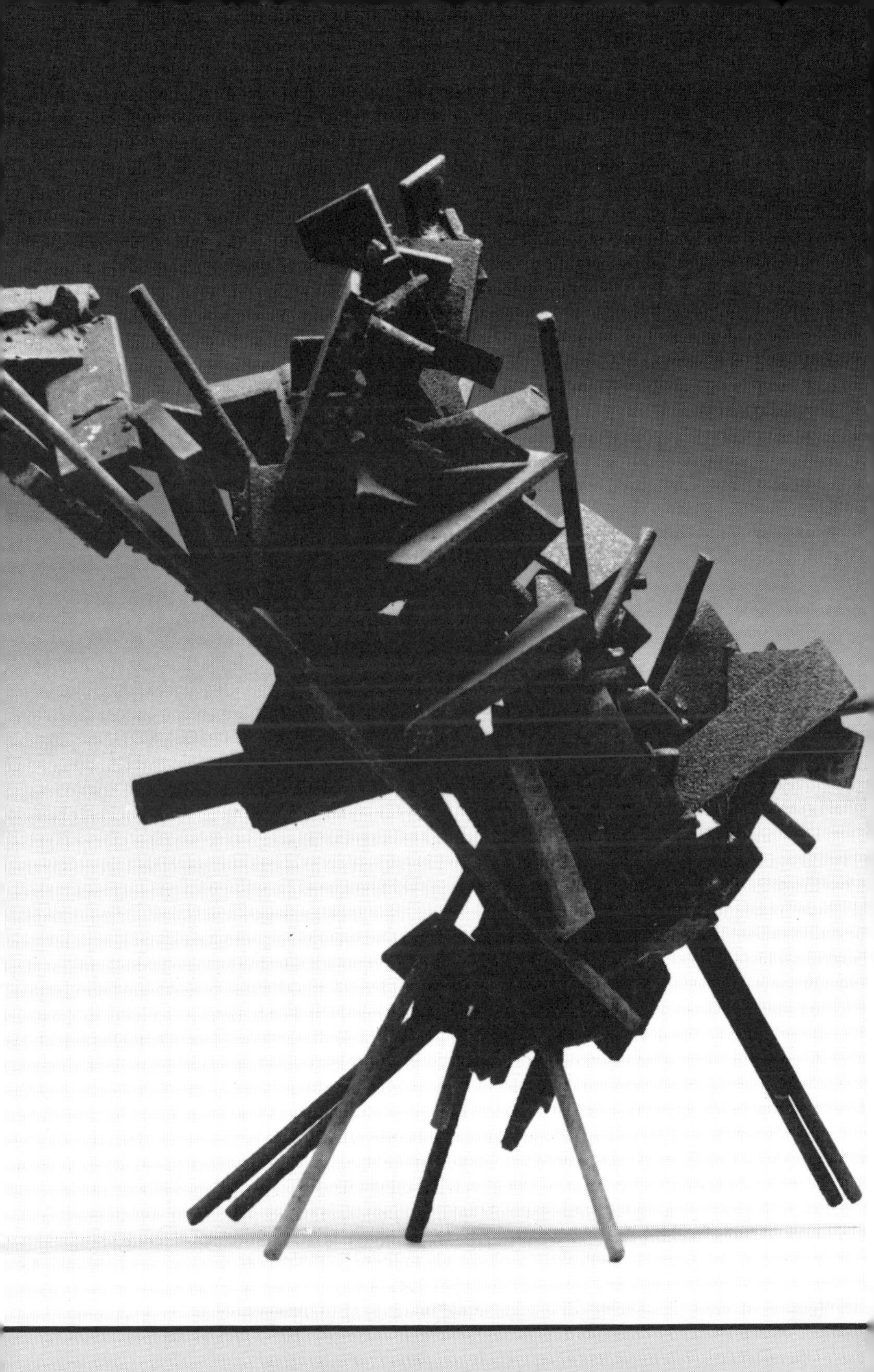

MEMORIAL TO GLENN GOULD

A WOMAN'S MASTERPIECE

She sculpts a statue
of her life,
caged in marriage,
caged in prose.

A stranger lurking
and foreseen
steals her child
from the floor,

writes a woman's
masterpiece
for the bookshelf
in the hall:

daughter bruised
behind an alley
garbage can,

clothing ripped
from infant skin
page by page by page.

HAMILTON BAY

The maple trees
around Hamilton Bay
rust a consummate leisure.
Rank, polluted waters mimic
in reflection a city's
easy tedium; grey towers
stare back at themselves,
vacant eyes interred
in a looking glass.

I do not know why seasons
die before we savour them.
What answer satisfies two
who died and decompose
beneath the rotting leaves,
mongrels running here?

It maybe takes a death
to persevere, a death held
high to rouse nativity. Even
branches robbed of foliage
embrace with moist serenity
the blue of sky for leaves.

How she perseveres to die
like September and die again
I cannot tell. The sun
on her face, beside the bay,
steals thinking from my body
like a kiss.

MEN ARE LIKE PIGS

inside a costume rental store
you receive the costume of a pig;
it is loose around the waist.

waiting at the slaughterhouse,
you are waiting in line.
no one has been here before.

you are killed and dismembered.

the butcher has a sale today.
he is selling your ribs to Eve.
she is driving home with a bag.

Eve is making you a stew.
she is cooking dinner in the nude.
she is wearing a costume.

BORDER POEM

We the Monroe-doctrined
of Canada

decline to share
the moon

or a Pulitzer prize
for the witch-hunter's art

or Pax Americana
bribing and starving the poor.

We beg you
to spare us

the born again of football fields
waving the Stars & Stripes

on Bible-
thumper's knees.

In a pinch
we'll fly down

to Disneyland,
compare with pagan eye

if Christ and John Wayne
are really one.

THE SINGING OF FAIRUZ

Given the sacrifice,
woman and man,

I still believe
her eyes are water on a star.

The moon, a devotion,
empties the night in her hair

and I walk naked-heeled
while darkness folds over villages.

The morning brings
a bitter sun to steal her, proves

the solitary fear
that she was only passing.

BEACH ROAD

They feed you
in segregated rooms
like bulls kept ready
for breeding. After
two beers
you bring down
the government.

Joy to you, laureate
of the tavern.
Blessing and joy
to your leather glove
and workshirt, to your
bargain store shoes
that dissolve
when it rains, to
your wife and unemployed

kids in stucco housing
all mortgaged
at twenty per cent.
And joyful benediction
on your lifetime
of credit.

It's 3:25. The day shift
has gone home
on the buses.

You order a draft
and with the patience
of steel
humour the college kid
Maoist. He
wants to be born
without living.

EDGAR

He looks through
the window,
wintry eyed,
scanning dregs
of January. Trees
outside
bend and vanish,
jagged turning
out of sight.
His eyes grow
full, dusty
sediment.

There's steam
on the walls, the
air is softly
aching. I wait,
he waits,
and life begins
to leave him.

FAMILY ALBUM

My father. The factory laid
invisible welts on his back,

drove him into the concrete floor
until he made jokes that smelled
of iron dust, dreamed of fishes,
the stream long dry.

My mother Anastasia, dispatched
among rigid, breaking immigrant
spines. At ten she could love
no more the blushing child's

movie screen, and lamented her
own mother's drudging decay,
vassal's wage, a slave
in Pennsylvania.

My farmer uncle, stinking and
content, a lifetime of harvest
tallied on his skin, his arm that
thrashed anything coarse or gentle.

Look at these pages.
I have no secret to conceal.

My people carried the rich
on nameless sagging backs
until they saw the world in black
and white, then yellowed with
age like photographs.

A MAN WHO COMES TO TERMS WITH EARTH

A man who comes to terms
with earth
needs more a dirge
than praise. Credos fester
on his tongue; he spits
a bitter, creamy phlegm,
his shield that carries
an arm. With
contempt for the time
of day, he shuts his eye
to rock and weed
he needs an unclosed
eye to see.

Sing the plowman
sunk to his knees in earth;
his back is forged,
an arch around the sun.
Yet he walks
a furrowed path
because the way is clear
on dusty fields
gutted in his name.
If he plowed an acre
of his heart,
found no terms with earth,
would the singing
know his name?

I too have plowed
a moist, rock-ridden terrain.
Once I gave up
the plow
I took a fallow field instead
for what I might have given
seed. There is no
harvest now.

A farmer walks unschooled
among the rich,
wears a suit to beg
an air of gentry in the town.
I ask him why he drags
his plow, what he knows
of earth. For mine was
but a blunt and angry blade
that broke to rust
like April in her tomb
of clay.

SUNDAY IN DACHAU

There are photographs
in Dachau: discarded
bodies, hollow stares
of fish on a plate,
lampshades tattooed.

Beyond mute foundations
where barracks stood,
a restaurant cook
renames anonymous flesh,
a tasty if greasy
cuisine. Yet

patrons drink blood,
and know they're drinking
blood. Over wurst they
offer reverent thanks,
a prayer that smells, it
smells of Sunday school

MILTON AVERY'S PAINTINGS

A massive rectangular sea
lingers over the beach,
rumbling aside
to my brain's darkest winter,

coming and going existences
walk the pastel grandeur,
smoking pink washes
made sand
in glacial presence of water,

two figures, obscure and
planetless, staple a ration
of landscape
to muffled green strokes,
the tide,

and at hand another painting:
the body is a temple,
walk in it.

Along the adjacent wall
a halycon river, elemental
black, pours death
into a goblet now spilling
a blinding
triangular light.

Whitney Museum, November 1982

SUZANNE FARRELL

She thinks for the tree

green on the northern side,
a wanderer lost might
save his skin,

southerly in her sleep,
branches aquiver.

She enchants the loveless
ritual: axes wild on the tree,

woodsmen sowing fears in blood,
their women apart
who own or die.

Her body unfolds, a season
of leaves where moon
and sun disappear.

A man need only cut her down
to know how long

the debt-divided heart
must wander on chance
for a pathway.

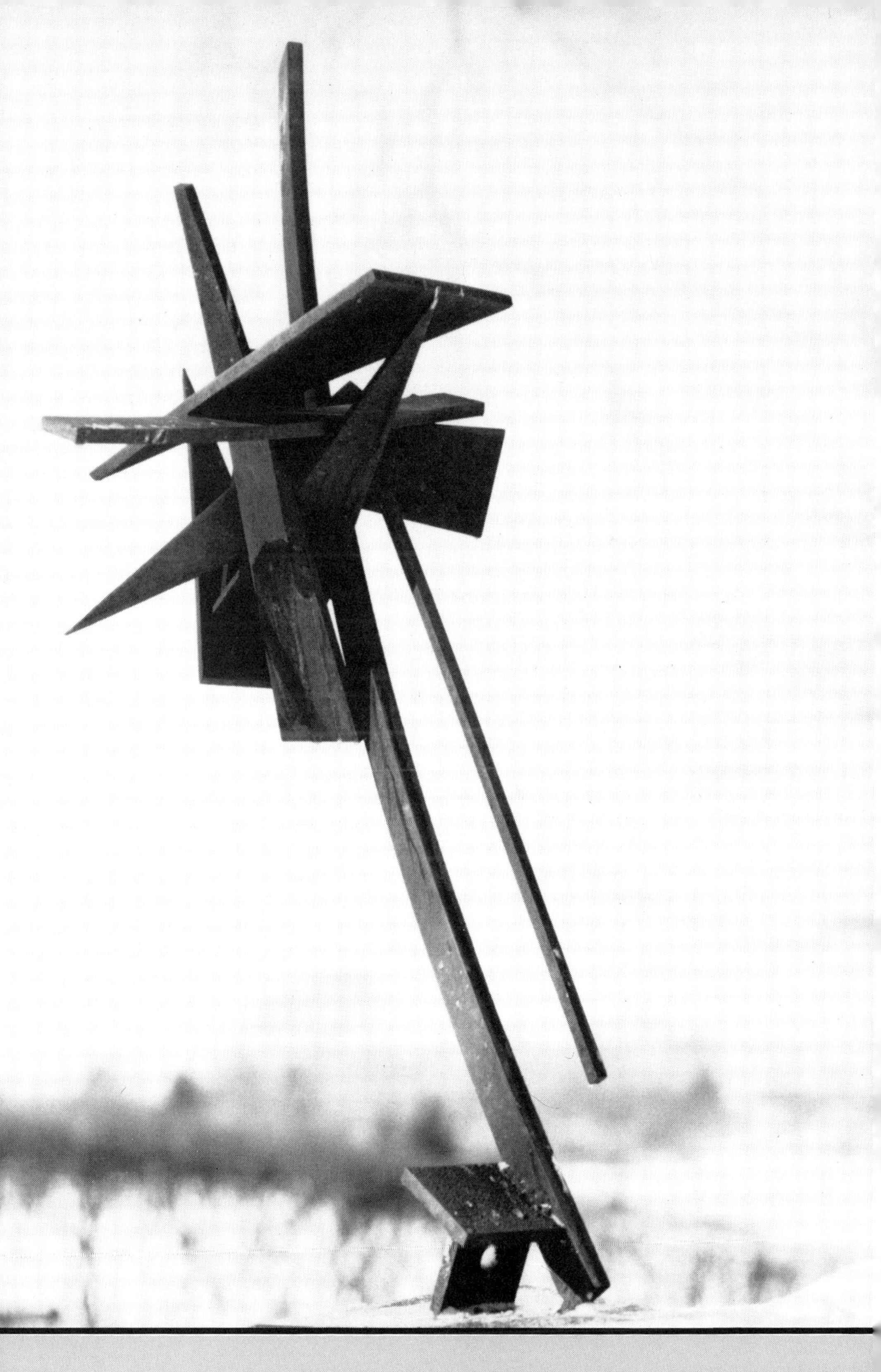

PAS DE DEUX

MARY

In a coffin
come to town

her delicate
body,
her laughter

crushed
on a highway
in France.

I remember
the kiss
of a dead

woman's mouth
when she was
alive

and we wore
her spunk
for a tempest.

ALI AKBAR KHAN

Daylight withers, a
sky's chilly gradation
pursuing the sun.
My thinking and twilight
combine.

No more the sunrise,
devotion woven to earth
, Raga Basant-Mookhari,

but night at hand
coffin-lidded on each man's
particular love. The

planet ends in grace,
a hymn to its beginning.

My body speaks a sun's
memory in the sweet
hesitation
of Raga Shree.

A HOUSEWIFE

She slices a tomato,

imagines her wrist
diameters of flesh,

nibbles the bugless
unchewable skin.

She has eaten her arm,
spit out the bone;

it's her husband
she broils in the oven.

IONIAN SEA

The Ionian Sea
tends his isolation.
The gull flies solo
over the tried and true

bidding ghosts
he seems to set at liberty
in flying free.

I would fly
beside the gull,
know the sun's meditation
in the depth
of this Grecian Sea.

But some consume
what a gull will not tell
for poison;
only the dead
live my world and their own.

Dear friend who sent me here,
why did you die
so young
and lonely as a gull?

for Bill, in memoriam

WHAT THE CELLS TELL US

What the cells tell us
is how to divide,
never to reason
with words indivisible.

Inside her touch I divided
though we like a cell
were dividing; she severed
word from cell, asked me,

wordless, to stay. Then I
unbridled, dividing,
bade her cease dividing
until she divided in clay.

DYING WOLF

The road
to your body
is paved,
slick with oil.
I hear
diesel trucks,
not the gurgling
of your lungs.

Come, dying wolf:

I will share
metaphysics
with you. I will
curse technology,
worship terrain
that is yours
for a grave
and mine no longer.

I will hunt
the hunter
who rides a snowmobile,
the one
who runs amuck
starved in need
of wonder, the one
I'd rather mourn
than love.

You will learn
another man's
mystery: your killer
will crawl to death
in his sport.

THE SCENE

"You're
making me
impotent,"

he said.

"I will
not tell
you,"

she said.

The setting:
there were
chairs

and a
gauntlet
of reasons
to continue.

RUE ST. DENIS

In the care of alleys
rotted men sleep,

every step is heard.

She descends,
her blunt, unflattered
age

nameless for the taking.

Streetlights and gutters
play witness

to the marketplace
body
of Les Halles,

painted and waiting,
a brazen corpse,

three pounds of her
for a franc.

She speaks to lure,
warm as guidebook prose;

in the doorway
her starlit hand
holds a key.

Paris

SWING SHIFT

punchclocks stoke
the furnaces:
hellmouth on schedule.
not a patriarch's town
(in the kingdom of steel
the ingot gives blessing)

young faces engraved
for mundane eternity,
negroid from dust,
confirming their talent
to sweat: the time
of day is indecent.

they curse the open
hearth to a whore
on the afternoon shift;
but immigrant words
cannot penetrate the
temper of animate steel.

IN AMSTERDAM

dancing
is like sex

laughed Fran

who danced
a perfect

simile

PROVENCE

The mistral swoops,
eternal scavenger,
on the Gypsy shrine
of Les Saintes Maries
de la Mer. Beside

the road
a dried up river bed:
web of memory,
gashes.

Van Gogh painted fiercely
this arid land

where bulls are tormented,
prayers whispered
by candlelight
to the black patron
saint. Van Gogh

made bold to take the sun
for a hue, burned
to a cinder for his pains.

What whim of earth
demanded this sacrifice?

desolate strokes of
a burning brush, incensed
yellow, purgatorial blue,

colours like scars
that healed on scars.

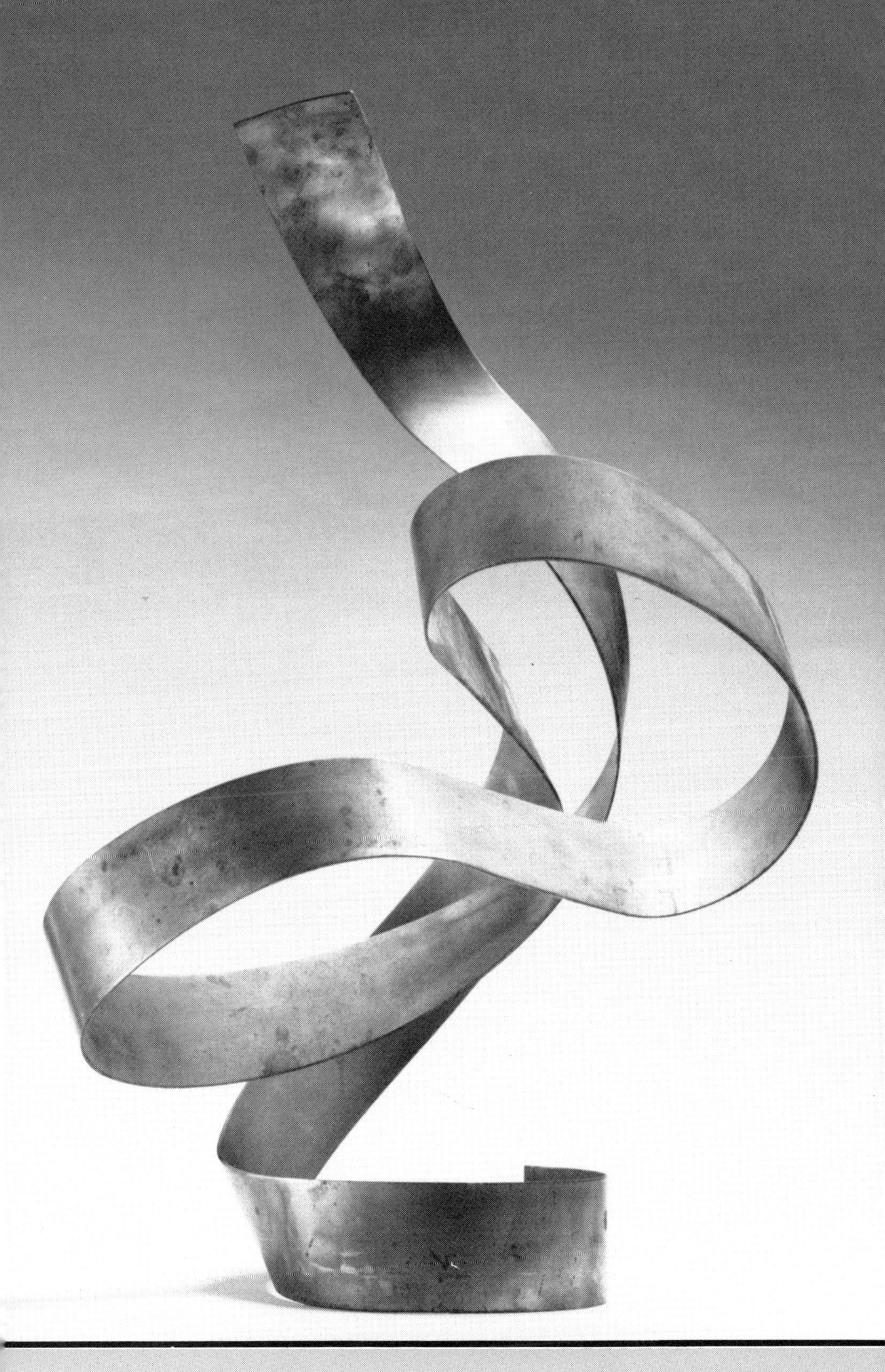

FLAMENCO

MADRID

Madrid has willed
a cruel sorcery
on this pilgrim
to Castilla.

5 minutes
from the Prado, almost
snoring back to back
with Goya's
Maja in the buff

the pension is cheap

but the pullchain
on the toilet snaps,
lands in my
nonchalant hand!

No way to cover up.

Three days later
on the train
north to Paris
I still feel cheated
by invention.

FOR THE WAITRESS

A Coltrane-ripping-skin
situation,
every note unwound,

your spartan glower
kicking up dirt,
I know the key.

I would improvise on you,

do tricks in the maze
of your skin,
confess my body in yours.

If you were less murky
of mood
I would sing in you solo,

rhythm and sax,
and bop with Bird
back to Kansas.

ANOTHER ZEN POEM

When the world divides
into hell and aesthetics,

I give my Oxford Dictionary
a boot in the ass
and kick it right out
of the language. Then I

flip through a book
by Suzuki on Zen.

I own ten books describing
mondos, koans and satori;
I keep them for DISPLAY.

It's hard to provide
an unbiased account
of the shock in our WASPy
neighbourhood

when a group of
authentic
Japanese
Zen
monks

pulled up in front of our
house in a rented Volkswagen
van, slipped through a crack
in my Gutenberg brain,

and read this poem, laughing.

A WINDLESS NIGHT

A windless night
yet wind in your hair
wine-scented laughter
my skin at high tide

A succulent kiss
your lips divide
pour wine through my body
my mouth opened wide

WOMEN LIKE YOU

In the presence
of each other
we lie to ourselves,

then we shape confession
like putty.

I should put a match
to the glossy whore
dangling in my sleep,

deliver my body some light.
But you are lawless
and beautiful;

women like you never learn
to give in.

You seduce all the men
around me, naked in your brain,
to endless lechery,

weigh our ego for ego
not balls,
giggle at our asses.

Damn your revenge!

I never burned a hag
with garlic in her tea.
I cut a slice of apple pie,

found myself a passenger
commuting to a garden.

OMARI BOROSO

Omari Boroso, wedding
musician, understands
a bridesmaid laughing;
young men follow him
through the marketplace
till he slices a dried up
leaf, carves a reed,
spits to the right, plays
the zumari.
He shapes a piercing
counterpoint to Ramadan: a
musician who reads women's
eyes and the stifling
religion of men
were never destined to let
each other be.
A gull above the shoreline
cuts a listless, elegant
design; bony cats pillage
these putrid, narrow streets,
claim what veiled women
discard to rot.
In time my thoughts obey
Boroso's melody
rising into the afternoon:
we live to die, move
from place to place.

Lamu & Nairobi, 1980

PAS DE MOI

I never died for love.
I ached my share,
a puppet pulling
strings. There are
witnesses, damage
was done.

But I try to keep busy,
abandon the part
of me that died
for the first snowfall,

see the ballet
believing swans would
pack it in for muted
lovers, plastic bouquets.

In my darkness I pluck
ballerinas from the stage
as you might seize
a butterfly from the air

just to let it go free
without the need
of wizardry. At curtain
call I leap on stage
to dance a pas de moi.

If a god of vanity
wants earth to heal
the crowded, loveless night

let him pay heed to ballet
where women glide
like lily pads in heat.

HOCKEY HAIKU

Men are like
the Toronto
Maple Leafs:

they lose,
they keep
selling out.

IMMIGRANTS

Lest we make them
the mouthpiece
of a gentler universe,
let us spare their names
the encumbrance
of legend.

They carried a suitcase
to Brazil, left
feudal Galicia undisturbed
by their going,
lost their only son
dead in a ditch,
would die themselves
before they had
forgotten.

When Amelia was born
he was drunk
in a tavern; his wife
got up to chop wood
for a fire. They
watched one daughter
give up her mind,
the others blistered
by the touch
of workingmen.

My grandmother died
in April, gasping for
air; my grandfather lived
to feel his arteries
turn to stone.

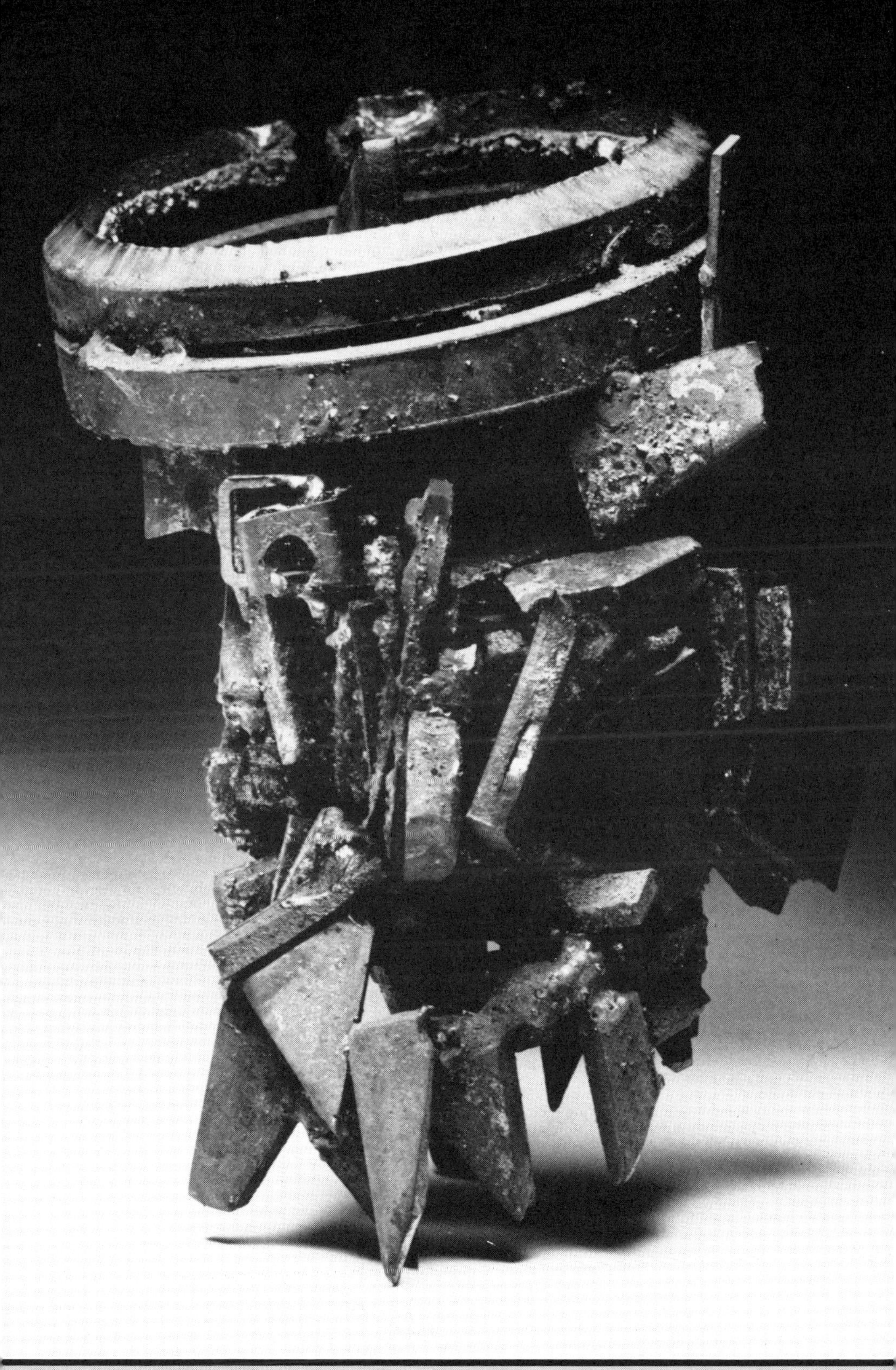

KING LEAR

Acknowledgements

I wish to extend my sincere thanks to the editors of the following
periodicals for first publishing poems, some now revised, from this
collection.

The Fiddlehead
Poetry Canada Review
Dalhousie Review
Quarry
Canadian Author & Bookman
Watchwords
True North/Down Under
Mamashee
The Globe and Mail
Waves
Scrivener
Poetry WLU
Poetry Toronto
The Canadian Literary Review
Tower
Gamut
Hamilton Cue Magazine
Origins
Pierian Spring
The Asianadian

The Antigonish Review

I feel equally grateful to the following: the Ontario Arts Council
for my temperamental typewriter, stamps, and vegetarian sustenance
by way of a timely grant; Mike Walsh, James Polk, Margaret
Strecker, Gérard Dion, and Dorothy Livesay for their much-valued
opinions; Peter Hogan for the blessing of his lens on my sculptures;
and especially Irving Layton, a man of consistent generosity,
who helped me uncloud some of these poems with his insight and
cloud his den with cigarillos.

THE SCULPTURES

1. BEETHOVEN: SYMPHONY NO. 9 IN D MINOR
   Welded steel — 40″x43″x20½″

2. MEMORIAL TO McLUHAN
   Welded steel — 14½″x11½″x11¾″

3. PAVLOVA
   Welded steel — 11¾″x46¼″x9½″

4. MEMORIAL TO GLENN GOULD
   Welded steel — 25″x21½″x15½″

5. PAS DE DEUX
   Welded steel — 45¾″x18″x31″

6. FLAMENCO
   Bent steel — 27″x18½″x16″

7. KING LEAR
   Welded steel — 10″x7″x9″

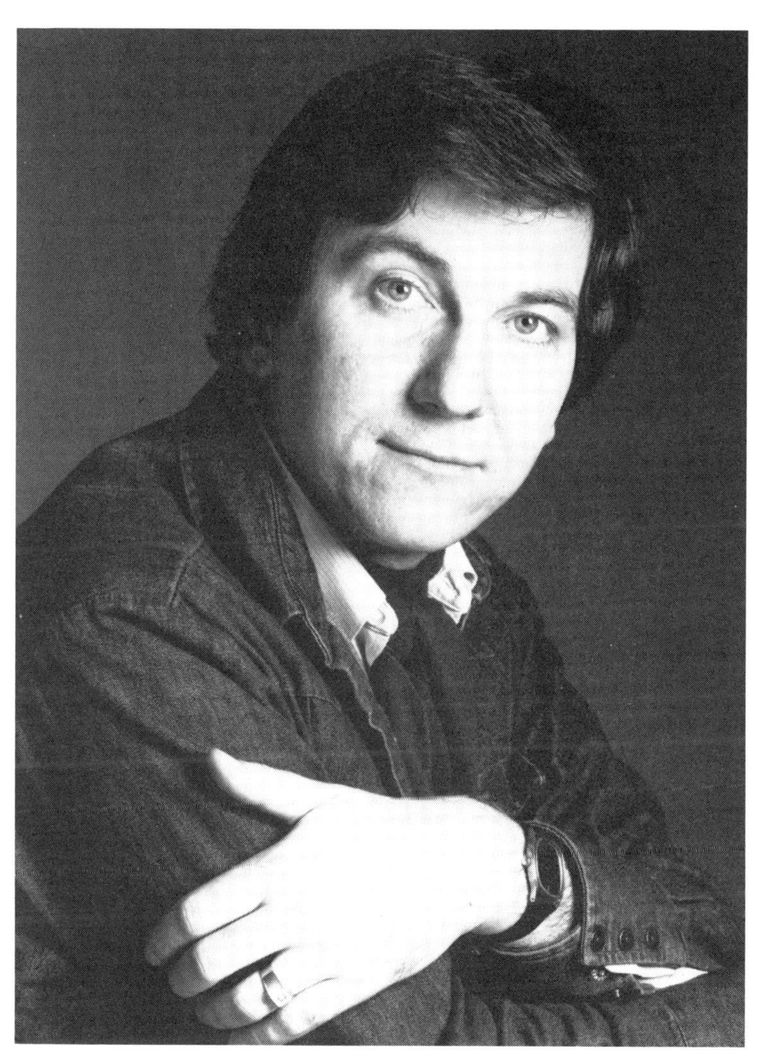

JAMES STRECKER